Home *in* Harmony

Home *in* Harmony

A Practical Guide to Organizing

ANDREA WAIT

Published 2023
Printed in the United States of America
Print: 979-8-9894049-0-2
E-book: 979-8-9894049-1-9
Library of Congress Control Number: 2023922031

Cover and interior design by Tabitha Lahr
Cover photos © Shutterstock.com

To my Mom, thank you for teaching me
the importance of making my bed every day.

Contents

Contents

Foreword

———— ⟨∞⟩ ————

When Andrea told me she was starting an organizing business in 2009, my first thought was, *Bingo! Of course you are.* Never mind that I had never heard of the profession. What I did know was that my friend always dove headfirst into solving any dilemma put before her—and quite often these predicaments involved perfect strangers who had the good fortune of having an issue in proximity to Andrea.

Andrea has a supreme knack for identifying a problem and tunneling through the extraneous matter to the heart of the solution. I've watched her do it day in and day out on organizing jobs for over a decade. But she was a clutter-buster from the day I met her twenty-two years ago, well before downsizing was on the lips of every health guru and streaming services had shows dedicated to her calling.

I was so honored when she asked if I would like to assist her when her business grew too big for one person in 2011, and again when asked to write this foreword. Of course, as I sat down at my computer I began to overthink how it would be possible to convey the journey we've shared in bringing tranquility and relief to so many households and business spaces. Then I channeled my inner Andrea—keep it simple!

Unlike my ramblings here, in the pages to follow you will find direct, no-nonsense instruction on how to create a calm and inviting environment in your home. This manual charts a precise course through problem areas in each of your living spaces, beginning with your own headspace, and will have you embracing your organizing challenges with calm and confidence.

I've seen the practical results Andrea's expertise brings for many gratifying years, so *congratulations*, dear reader, and welcome to the beginning of your new chapter.

—Nicoll Turner, Professional Organizer

Introduction

Dear reader,
Hello and welcome to my practical guide to organizing your home.

Perhaps you are at that point of life where you need help organizing but are not quite ready to get outside help. You believe you can still do this yourself. Kudos to you. Hopefully this book can give you some direction. Just like a manual for an appliance, this can be your guide to organizing your home.

Now is the time to learn how to navigate your way out of all the stuff that clutters your life to a place that brings you joy, contentment, and happiness. I'm no organizing royalty—neither Mari Kondo nor Peter Walsh. I am simply Andrea Wait—a regular person who has been in the organizing business for the last fifteen years. Along the way, I have seen the challenges so many of us encounter as we try to keep our lives clutter-free. With a daily influx of stuff, how do we learn to let go? It's a process.

Now, full disclaimer here: This book is not for everyone. Some people feel comfortable in spaces filled with things. But if you are like me and get that feeling of bliss when you walk into a freshly cleaned hotel room, this book is for you.

As a professional organizer, I am often asked the question, "Who is your worst client?" But there is no "worst" client; each of us has their own unique obstacles to overcome. The bottom line for the majority of us is that we just have too much stuff. If you are feeling overwhelmed, I can pretty much guarantee it is because you have more than you could ever want, need, or use.

I've had the pleasure of working helping clients all over the US, from New York to San Francisco, declutter their lives. In this book, I will share with you my professional experiences and will offer you suggestions and solutions to help you declutter yours. I know firsthand that the outcome can be life-changing. So please have an open mind and take this journey with me. You may be pleasantly surprised by the outcome.

Organizing needs cover the gamut—from seniors who need to downsize to young families making space for kids, and everything in between. There is no one-size-fits-all when it comes to "getting organized," but there are some basic principles. Your home should serve as a respite from the challenges of daily life. If yours isn't doing that for you, it's time to get it there. We are going to turn chaos into serenity.

I am not going to get into the nuts and bolts of the *whys* of your situation—why you are disorganized, why you hold on to things, or why things have ended up the way they have—in this book. Instead, I am going to offer you tangible solutions.

While we are on that topic: Do you have owner's manuals for items you already know how to operate—for example, your refrigerator, your toaster oven, your vacuum cleaner? If so, get up right now and throw them in your recycling bin! Look at that; you just had your first organizing win.

You don't have to read this entire book; just pick a section and then follow the steps. As you do so, I hope you find tips that not only tell you what to do but also inspire you to take action. My husband once asked me, regarding organizing cluttered homes, "Where do you start?"

My answer: "With the first thing I see."

Andrea Carr, professional organizer and daughter of well-known author and organizer David Carr, said it perfectly:

"Just do what's in front of you and do it well. It's a series of small acts performed over and over. It's the little things that make it better."

PART I:

Laying *the* Groundwork

CHAPTER 1:

Why Organize?

For me, the biggest motivation to get started on an organizing project is the anticipation of what can happen when the project has been completed. Even after all these years, I am still amazed by how life-changing the results can be . . . in the best ways. Here are just a few things people have told me about the benefits of organizing.

1. All of my belongings now have a home. My apartment feels so much bigger and I feel a hundred pounds lighter. I actually look forward to coming home and feeling the open and clean energy of my space.
2. I experienced a feeling of relaxation I haven't known in a long time. We made a messy, dysfunctional kitchen into a space that flows easily. There is more room for everything now, and I have what I need on hand, where I need it.

3. Knowing where everything goes seems obvious but in my house that was not the case. Ask anyone where an item lived and we all had a different response. Now we don't think twice about where we keep the scotch tape.

4. Our closets and kitchen are finally how they should be. Everything has a place and the clutter is gone. It has helped put me more at ease with the baby coming so soon!

5. I can't believe it but I am saving money now that my house is organized. Why? Well, I often would get frustrated trying to find something and would just give up and order a new one . . . everything from a pair of scissors to the dog's leash. And later on, of course, I would find said lost item.

6. Having a clean and organized home office has helped me to stay on track with my work and helped me with overall time management . . . fewer "I can't find that file" problems.

7. My children's teacher told me that my daughter, age six, and my son, age nine, were very smart but very disorganized. With our organization process in place, we now model what goes on in the classroom—e.g., take things out and then put them away. Both of their teachers say there has been a remarkable improvement with both kids. Best of all, we no longer have the morning shouting match about where my son last left his eyeglasses. I love the quiet of the morning now.

8. I think I look better because my house looks better and I am less afraid if someone just

randomly pops by. I no longer have to pretend
that I am not at home.

Do you see yourself in one of these scenarios? If
so, this book is for you!

CHAPTER 2:

Organizing Prep

————— ❧ —————

In order to ensure that your organizing session is successful, I suggest taking the following steps to get yourself ready:

1. Block out time on your calendar so there are no interruptions—no phone calls, no darting out to run errands, etc.
2. Get bags and boxes for donation. If you are someone who has accumulated many reusable shopping bags, this is your time to use those for donation bags and reduce your volume.
3. Get garbage bags for trash.
4. Contact your local charity shops to verify hours and what items they will accept.
5. If you have large pieces of furniture that you are ready to donate, schedule pickup of those items on organizing day.
6. If you think you will have many refuse items, contact one of your local junk hauling

companies and schedule a pickup for the end of the scheduled organizing day. Trust me, once you have gone through the organizing process you will be happy to have these folks come and take your junk away.

7. If you want stuff to leave your house as quickly as possible as you declutter and organize, consider posting the items you're shedding to the "free stuff" page on Craigslist. You can post your things in real time and simply put them out in front of your home for pickup. You will be amazed at how quickly items will go away! Remember at the end of the day to take your posting down and to remove any remaining items that are not taken, so you don't waste anyone's time or annoy your neighbors with a cluttered-up sidewalk.

8. Walk around your house and make note of areas where items are stored on the floor—books, blankets, electronics. Consider getting better storage, such as bookshelves and trunks for storage. You can often find these items on Craigslist and Facebook Marketplace.

9. Decide what you want to organize and read this book's room-specific chapters in advance to see if there is anything you might need to help make your project a success.

10. Tell a close friend that you are going to organize your home. This extra step may just keep you accountable to getting the project done—so you don't wake up on organizing day and decide to put it off.

CHAPTER 3:

The Three Whats

———————⬥———————

M y approach to every organizing project I do is to be systematic and methodical. I begin by creating an organized plan of attack — and that starts with answering three important questions:

1. What is your goal?
2. What is the intention of the space?
3. What is your deadline for completing the task?

What is your goal?

I believe it is imperative at the beginning of every organizing project to ask yourself what is that you want to achieve, the more specific the better. Goals can help you focus on next steps and can help you move in the direction you want to go in — toward a clutter-free, orderly life. Why is this important? Because halfway through your organizing project, you may begin to run out of steam, so having that clear goal—something like, *I want my family to be able sit down at our dining table and have a shared meal together*—may be enough to keep you going.

What is the intention of the space?

For every task you do, it is key to ask yourself the intention behind it. The decision-making process can frequently be overwhelming, so as you look at each item, your decision about whether something stays or goes should be based on, *Does this item fit the intention of the space?* I remember the first clients I worked for stored dog food in their office. What is the intention of an office? Not to feed the dog!

What is your deadline for completing the task?

The number one rule of organizing is to complete what you start. I can't tell you how many clients I have worked with who've told me they've made many attempts to organize, gotten to about the 90 percent mark, and then stopped. What happened next was that in their feelings of defeat regarding the remaining 10 percent, their cluttered chaos became even worse than it had been when they started. When we impose a deadline on ourselves, we hold ourselves accountable to finish the entire project—an absolute must if you want a clutter-free, organized home.

CHAPTER 4:

Clear Your Mind

———— ⌑ ————

Most of us want to jump right in and tackle the physical clutter, but I believe the first step here is to address the mental clutter. I believe when the mind is clear we make better choices and are less likely to become overwhelmed by the task at hand. Removing those obstacles makes the physical work that much easier.

How can we do that? I suggest practicing a simple meditation: a simple technique called 4-7-8 breathing. Here's how it works:

1. Turn off your phone.
2. Sit down in a comfortable chair and close your eyes.
3. Take a deep breath and place your feet flat on the floor; feel where your feet make contact with the ground beneath you.
4. Take a deep breath in for one, two, three, four seconds.

5. Hold for one, two, three, four, five, six, seven seconds.
6. Exhale for one, two, three, four, five, six, seven, eight seconds.
7. Repeat this cycle four times.

When I practice 4-7-8 breathing, in just a short amount of time I find I am calmer and more focused . . . two things key to effective organizing.

CHAPTER 5:

Face Your Fears

————— ❧ —————

N
ow that you have meditated and cleared your mind, let's address a big emotion that can prevent us from taking on the home organizing challenge: fear.

Irrational thoughts and fears are distractions that not only prevent us from completing this process but also, in many cases, even getting started. Here are some of the common ones that I have heard over the years:

What if I throw away something that I'll need in the future?

Instead of living in a world of "what if," ask yourself a different question: *What are the things that are important to me that I don't want to lose?* Prior to organizing, move those items to a safe place. Aside from those important keepsakes, remember, chances are that even if you do end up needing something you've gotten rid of somewhere down the line, you can almost certainly replace it then.

I can't donate any gifts my mom gave me; I don't want to hurt her feelings.

If you are truly worried about hurting her feelings, think about a way to use and incorporate the gift into your life. But more importantly, figure out a way to redirect your mom so that you don't get future gifts you don't want. Perhaps you can keep an ongoing list of items you actually need; or, if you want to avoid accumulating stuff, have her contribute to a fund that you can use for experiences like dinners out, movie tickets, and travel packages.

I can't get rid of that; I spent good money on it.

I love this saying. Does it also mean we sometimes spend bad money? I believe if you have purchased something and have not used it, you have experienced what I call "a purchase fail." My advice: Let it go. You don't use it. Donate it. And now *learn* something from that purchase fail.

For the longest time, I bought myself clothes that I never wore. I had an image of myself wearing bright, colorful clothes—but you know what? That is not me. I am a white T-shirt and blue jeans girl. I like pretty plain clothes. Sure, I still see clothes in a store window and think *Wow, that's cool,* even today—but now I have the presence of mind to remind myself, *And that's so not me.* This is your opportunity to get to know yourself and to practice exercising intentionality in your purchases. Not only will you reduce the amount of stuff you bring in the home, you will also reduce how much you need-lessly spend.

I may want that item again.

For these "one day I might use this" items, I suggest creating a timeline. You can either attach a label with a date to the item or put a reminder on your calendar to check if you have used it. Make a commitment to yourself that when the date is up, if you haven't used it, you will let it go.

I hate this gift from my friend, but what if she asks about it?

In all my years of organizing, I have never had a client who said this actually happened to them. But hey, if this is your fear, then let's focus on a solution:

Wear it. Display it. Photograph it and send that photo, accompanied by a thank-you, to your friend. And then, in time, let it go.

As you can see, fears are just rationalizations that prevent us from taking action. Instead of focusing on the fears of loss, focus on the possibility of what can come. I believe that when we let go of things that no longer serve us, we create the space for what does.

So let's let go of being afraid and just get started. And if you can't do that, then just go ahead and do it scared. You got this.

PART II:

Room *by* Room,
Category *by* Category

CHAPTER 6:

The Bedroom

———— ❧ ————

Okay, you are now ready to organize your home. In each chapter of this section, we will ask the Three Whats — *What is your goal? What is your intention for the space? What is your deadline for completing the task?* I suggest you take some time to answer each one prior to starting the actual work. Your responses should help you stay on track as you move through the project at hand.

Now, one of the first questions I often get is, "Where do I start?" My first choice in organizing a home is to start with the bedroom. I think this is one of the most important rooms in the house, as it is the place we go for rest, relaxation, and rejuvenation, and yet this is a room that often becomes the dumping ground for all sorts of stuff.

So let's get going!

Questions to answer:

1. What is your goal?
2. What is the intention of the space?
3. What is your deadline for completing the task?

Top Ten Recommended Organizing Tools

1. Slim felt hangers
2. Large clear storage containers
3. Masking tape and marker for labeling containers
4. Drawer dividers for your dressers, bathroom drawers, kitchen drawers, and any other drawers used for grouped items
5. One box, with dividers, for each person in your house (we'll get to why in Chapter 15!)
6. Bookshelves
7. Dressers
8. Clear shoe boxes and/or shoe shelves
9. Shelving units—garage, basement, pantry, deep closets
10. Garbage bags

Organizing your bedroom:

1. Walk around your room and take photos of everything—the room, the closets, the floors.
2. Make the bed. (Do you see how instantly this changes the feel of the room?) You can now use this large, flat surface as a sorting and organizing area.
3. Remove all items that do not meet the intention of the room. For example, paperwork and

bills do not belong in the bedroom. Important: Don't get too caught up in organizing those items. Instead, just take them to the location where they belong. We will get to organizing them later.

4. Remove all items in the room that no longer serve any purpose. For example, if you have large items, such as a chair, a couch, or a treadmill, that has just become a resting place for stuff, move that out of the room. Again, what is the intention of a chair in the room? A chair is for sitting on—so if it has become nothing more than a place to dump your clothes on, then it is not fulfilling its purpose. It is only making the room more cluttered.

5. Get everything off the floor and out from under the bed, then ask yourself, *Do these items fit the intention of the room?* If not, then either get rid of them or find them a better home. Hopefully by the time we're done decluttering, you will have so much space elsewhere that you will no longer need to store things under the bed.

6. Clean off your nightstand. This is another piece of furniture that can be a dumping ground—both on top and in any drawers. What is the intention of this nightstand? Yes, it's a great place for a reading lamp, a glass of water, or a book—but only those items should live there, nothing else. Things not in keeping with its intention must go.

7. Clear off all furniture surfaces. I love the expression "Keep flat surfaces flat." To me,

this is the gold standard of organizing; for many, however, it's impossible. If you *must* have something on top of your dresser, then just have one type of item: only pictures; only plants; only jewelry sorters. When you mix categories on surfaces, what you put on them quickly turns into a mixture of random stuff and becomes a cluttered mess.

8. Once you have removed everything that doesn't belong, it is time to do some good old-fashioned housework: vacuuming, dusting, emptying your trash bin. If possible, open a window or light a candle when you're done; enjoy what is now the serenity and beauty of your room!

9. Now that you have organized, purged, and cleaned it is time to put everything in its respective place. If your room services many purposes—reading, exercise, and crafting, for example—then designate specific zones for those items and put each thing in its new home.

10. Now that the bedroom is organized, it is time to tackle the clothes in your dressers and closets.

Now for your clothes and shoes:

In the US, it is said that people wear 20 percent of their clothing 80 percent of the time—and yet our closets are maxed out. Let's do something about that.

The easiest way to manage your clothes is to reduce their volume. Now, the idea of getting rid of clothes may sound scary—but remember, we're here to face our fears. Imagine if every time you looked into your closet or your drawers, it was easy for you to pick something out that you wanted to wear? That means everything in your wardrobe fits you and you like everything you see. *That* is a success.

Organizing your clothes:

1. Clear off the bed, again!
2. Set up a donation area and a garbage area with bags and boxes.
3. Take out ALL of your clothes (yes, I mean all of them) and group them into like categories — shirts, pants, dresses, jackets, etc. You can use your bed to sort. (When organizing, things tend to get worse before they getter better. I know it's a mess right now. Have faith that it will get better if you stick with it.)
4. It's decision time. Remove all items that are torn, stained in bad condition and put in garbage bag.
5. Remove all the items that you consider old or out of fashion and put them in a donation bag.
6. Remove all the items that don't fit you and put them in a donation bag. I know this is tricky for people, so if there are some items that you absolutely love, you can keep them—but if you do, you must have a timeline for how long you will hold on to them. It has been my experience that when we hold on to items that are too small and they are kept front-and-center in our closets, we are almost shaming ourselves. The goal is to get dressed, and keeping ill-fitting items can hold us back. I have been told by many that *after* letting go of those

too-small clothes is when the weight came off, and when that happened they were excited to buy something new, not regretful about letting go of the old items.

7. Now decide what to keep. Choose what fits you, what you know you wear, and what you absolutely love.

8. Before putting things away, wipe down the inside of dresser and clean your closet.

9. Put the "keep" items back into the closet and/ or drawers by category.

10. You may still have items left on the bed. I call that your "maybe" pile. Before you put them away, take a look at your pretty closet and drawers and ask yourself: *Am I really going to wear these? Do I really need, really want to keep these items?* If the answer is yes, put them away. If the answer is no, put them in a donation bag.

11. Now take a good look again at your slimmed-down closet and drawers. Hopefully, you can and will wear every item you kept.

12. Time to move on to shoes!

Organizing your shoes:

1. Go get all of your shoes and sort them into categories—sneakers, dress shoes, etc.

2. Remove any shoes that hurt and put them in a bag for donation.

3. Remove any shoes that are damaged or stained beyond repair and put them in the trash.

4. Group duplicate shoes. Put the pair you no longer wear in your donation bag.

5. Grab the shoes that you regularly wear. Put them in your "keep" pile.
6. Any shoes left? Ask yourself if you have another pair of shoes in your "keep" pile that serves the same purpose as the ones you're considering. If so, put them in your donation bag.
7. Clean the area where you will keep your shoes. Put your shoes away, organized by category. As for storing your shoes, you can use stackable shoe shelves or clear box containers. I personally like the container boxes, as they keep my shoes clean and I can see all of them.
8. Take photographs of your bedroom, your clothes and shoes. Post to your favorite social media page. You should be very proud of yourself. Job well done!

Handling donations:

Congratulations, now that you have organized your bedroom, your clothes, and your shoes, it is time to complete the project. Take your donation bags out of the house immediately and drop them off at a donation center. This is the most important part of the organizing project and my biggest rule . . . COMPLETE WHAT YOU HAVE STARTED! I have found that people who do not complete this part of the project start to reincorporate the items they were willing to get rid of, adding clutter back to their recently organized space.

Sell your items rather than donating them is an option, of course. If you decide to sell, make sure you follow through with this task. Check out your local consignment stores in advance by calling to see what they are looking to buy. You can also explore selling on online sites like Poshmark, eBay, and ThredUp, as well as your local Facebook Marketplace page.

But remember, your goal is to *get organized* — so if the process to sell becomes too overwhelming, consider donating. Not only is it a gift to someone else, it is a gift to yourself . . . the gift of freedom from all that stuff that's been weighing you down!

When donating, group like items together into individual bags/boxes: clothes, shoes, household items, books. This makes the drop-off process simple for you, and for those who will be processing your donations.

Tips for keeping your bedroom organized:

- Make your bed every day.
- Have only two sets of sheets for each bed — one set goes on the bed and one set is in the closet and can be used for laundry rotation.
- Pick up things off the floor and either hang them up or put them in the laundry basket.
- Have a system for laundry. I like the three-bag separating cart (cold, warm, hot water); when one bag is full, it goes directly into the wash.
- Leave your room how you would like to return to it later.
- Relocate things that don't belong in the room daily.
- Clear the floor; clear the surfaces. On repeat.
- If you are donating large pieces of furniture, look into your local charity shops, as many provide pickup services.
- Have you ever seen a random shopping cart

out in the supermarket parking lot on your way into the store—and then later, upon returning to your car, noticed that more carts, along with some other random junk, joined that original cart while you were inside shopping? Yep, we do that at home. One random item comes into the bedroom—maybe a piece of mail or some snacks—and then, over time, the pile grows. That's the law of attraction. Be careful about what you bring into each room.

When your room is organized . . . things my clients have said:

I now feel at peace. I can walk through my closet again, and I can see very clearly where everything is.

I can't tell you how much relief I get from looking into my closet and knowing every item of clothing fits. I no longer feel bad about clothes that don't fit. Getting dressed in the morning has become a pleasure. Imagine every item in your closet fitting and you will like it.

Every time I walk into my closet, I smile.

When I walk into my bedroom after a hectic day I get a feeling of inner peace as I look at my made bed and clutter-free floor. I no longer feel that my bedroom door needs to be closed; instead, it is inviting me to come in.

Easy let-go items:

That random chair stacked with clothes that you need to put away. Clothes that don't fit. Shoes that hurt your feet.

Craziest thing I ever saw:

I once had a client who stored boxes of previous pets' ashes in his closet. When he told me he didn't have a lot of space in his closet to put his clothes, I told him, "I think I found some space." I moved the boxes of ashes to a small shelving unit in his bedroom, which freed up space for his baseball hats, scarves, and gloves.

When you are storing things like ashes, make a space that dignifies and honors rather than hides . . . or at least, don't stash them away in your clothes closet. That's for clothes.

CHAPTER 7:

The Kitchen

———————◦⚓◦———————

For many, the kitchen is the second most important room in the house. It is a place for creativity and connection and, most importantly, nourishment. Our kitchen plays a major role in healthy living. Let's create a space that reflects your goals for living your best life.

Questions to answer:

1. What is your goal?
2. What is your intention for the space?
3. What is your deadline for completing the task?

Dear Andrea,
I see all of your amazing reviews on Yelp and although I am nervous about the idea of organizing, I know it is time. If you had to say in a very simple way, why are so many of us overwhelmed by all of this?
Thanks,
Sally

Dear Sally,
I like your direct question and so I will give you a direct answer. Why are we so overwhelmed? Sally, I think when asked this question, 99.99999 percent of all organizers will have the same answer: We have too much stuff! We are a consumer-driven society, and consuming has been made incredibly easy by services like home delivery. So for someone like yourself who is feeling overwhelmed, I would say that step one is to start paying attention to what is coming into your house regularly. When it comes to my stuff, I am a fan of the 3 R's: reduce, reuse, recycle. Reduce the amount that I bring in. Reuse by wearing repeat outfits at special events. Recycle . . . I love, love, love dropping off bags of donation items. I feel lighter every time I drive away.

And if you're thinking you want to actively take on an organizing project, I suggest that instead of getting bogged down by the enormity of trying to do it all, you should pick one small project that you know you can conquer, which can be as small as,

I am going through my shoe collection and I am going to get rid of all shoes that don't fit or that hurt my feet, and that I know I will never wear. Starting with a win might help you to keep going, and eventually it just might not seem so overwhelming. Thanks for your question,
Andrea

Prepare to organize your kitchen:

1. Divide this job into two categories: food and nonfood.
2. Clear off all surfaces—tables and counters—so you can you use them for sorting.
3. Get boxes and garbage bags for donations and discarded items.

Organizing non-food items:

1. Set up a donation/discard area with the garbage bags and boxes.
2. Take "before" photographs.
3. Remove all items that do not meet the intention of the room.
4. Pull out all non-food items and group them into categories: dishes, glasses, mugs, pots and pans, silverware, cooking tools, etc.
5. Per category, decide how many items you really need—e.g., do you really need twelve champagne glasses when you don't ever drink it or serve it?

6. Identify obvious items you don't use and put them in a donation box.

7. Identify items that "have seen better days"—meaning they're broken, chipped, rusted, or stained—and throw them away.

8. Identify duplicate items. Pick the one that is the best and then put the extra item in a donation box.

9. Consider posting "go-away" items on Craigslist's "free stuff" page and put them outside for immediate pickup.

10. Decide where everything should live and what makes the most sense to you. Use one section of the cabinets for food and the other section for non-food items such as silverware, plates, cups, and small appliances. All kitchens are different, so decide what works best for you. I personally like dividing my kitchen into two sections—food items and non-food items and then within those grouping things by category.

11. To optimize your storage capacity, move shelves up or down so that more shelves may be added. Take an existing shelf to a hardware store to have more shelves cut. Then space each shelf out to accommodate the size of the items in each category. You will be amazed at how much more of one category can live in a cabinet when you get more shelves and maximize your use of your vertical space. You'll no longer need to stack your mugs on top of each other!

12. Wipe down cabinets and shelves. Throw away cabinet liners; they are just traps for crumbs and dirt. Instead, once a month take a damp

towel or cleaning cloth and wipe everything down. Not only will you keep everything clean, but this will also be an opportunity to repeat steps 3 and 4.

13. Put everything away.

Organizing food items:

1. Pull out all food and drinks from cabinets, closets, and drawers.
2. Group items into categories.
3. Throw out expired food.
4. Throw out food that does not meet your nutritional goals.
5. Wipe down shelves and cabinets, and the inside of your refrigerator, microwave, and stove.
6. Decide where everything should live and what makes the most sense.
7. Put everything away. I like having specific zones in cabinets, e.g., pasta in one place, canned goods in another, condiments in still another, and so on.

Final steps to kitchen organization:

1. Take "after" photos of everything and post to social media . . . celebrate a job well done!
2. Take your throw-away items out to the trash and bring your donation items to their destination.

What can I do with all the food and kitchen items I am getting rid of?

Contact your look food bank and shelters to see if they are taking any donations, both food items as well as kitchen goods.

Kitchen goods can also be donated to your local Goodwill. I personally love Goodwill, as they train and employ people who often are overlooked for employment. But make sure before to check their list of what they take before attempting to drop off items.

Tips for keeping your kitchen organized:

- Keep spices in a drawer and lay them down label-up so they are easy to see and therefore will be used. There are a variety of sorters that can be placed in drawers for organizing spices.
- Keep large cooking utensils in a wide-mouth jar to free up drawers and prevent the collection of more stuff.
- Be careful about buying in bulk—both food and non-food items. Unless you are living in the wilderness, you don't need enough pantry items to sustain you for six months.
- You say your kitchen is small and your cabinets are full. I take that to mean that you have too much food. Do you know what happens when your cabinets are full of canned soup, canned beans, canned whatever? You no longer can see what you have—and eventually, these food items expire and have to be tossed. Start taking inventory of what you eat and replace that. I mean, really, why are you stocking up on food

as if the grocery store is about to disappear? If you find you have expired food while you do your clean-out, this is your wake-up call to stop over-buying.

- Decide how much you need for each type of item. If you are a family of four, do you need twelve coffee mugs?

- What's with all the tea? I can't tell you how many homes I enter that have a cabinet stuffed with tea boxes. It is time for you to stop buying tea. Drink what you have. Decide what you like, and then only buy that. Once in a while, when the tea box is empty, try a new flavor. Pay attention to anything you have an abundance of; commit to using it, and if you don't . . . say bye-bye to that.

- Make sure you take a look at your kitchen cabinets to see if you can move the shelves according to the height of each grouping; when you have more space, go get yourself some more shelves. Maximize your storage.

- At the end of each meal, clean the kitchen. Wash dishes and cookware and then put them away. Put everything back where it belongs. At the end of the day, make sure the countertops are wiped down and the floor is swept. Imagine walking into a clean kitchen in the morning. Start practicing leaving a space for how you want it to be when you enter it the next day, and you will stay organized.

When your kitchen is organized . . . things my clients have said:

We made a messy, dysfunctional kitchen into a kitchen that flows with ease. There is more room for everything now; I have what I need on hand, where I need it. I love the way.

I had a dinner party and my guests couldn't believe how organized everything was; my kitchen was a delight to cook in.

Easy let-go items:

Expired food and food that doesn't meet your dietary needs.

Craziest thing I ever saw:

Well, I don't know how it ranks on the crazy scale, but this to me ranked as "so not the place to store this." I was organizing the kitchen—specifically, the pots and pans cabinet. Out of the corner of my eye, toward the back of the cabinet, I noticed light blue boxes. I thought, *Huh, why would someone store Tiffany jewelry boxes in their kitchen?*

Sure enough, not only had my client stored her jewelry in the cabinet, she had also *forgotten they were there.*

That's what happens when we put our stuff in random places instead setting intentions for where everything should live.

CHAPTER 8:

The Bathroom

———— ❧ ————

I am always amazed by how many random things end
up getting stored in the bathroom. The room we go
into in order to get clean can often be the dirtiest room
in the house — think stuffed drawers and cabinets filled
with opened tubes of off ointments and lotions that have
left a sticky, gooey, mess.

For me, this is the easiest room to practice minimalism
in. I have just what I need and nothing else.

Questions to answer:

1. What is your goal?
2. What is your intention for the space?
3. What is your deadline for completing the task?

Organizing your bathroom:

1. Take "before" photos.
2. Set up trash bags and donation bags and boxes.
3. Clear off the countertop to use for organizing.
4. Empty all the cabinets and drawers, the tub, and the shower.
5. Remove all items that do not fit the intention of the room.
6. Group all like items: medicine, beauty products, dental products, hair products, soaps, lotions, paper products, cleaning products, and towels.
7. Do you have any items that are empty, expired, or unusable? Throw those away. *Do not* keep old medicine "just in case"—use it or lose it. The old medications can be dropped off at your local pharmacy for proper disposal.
8. From each group, pull out all the items that are currently in use and decide the best place for each group to live.
9. Remove all items that you no longer use—e.g., shavers, hair dryers, and accessories—and put them in a donation box.
10. If you have duplicate items, pick the one you use the most (or like the most) and donate the rest.
11. If you have back-up bathroom supplies, consider storing them in one specific area. If bathroom storage is limited, consider using other spaces, like where you store towels. I like to call this your "home store." Use clear shoeboxes to store like items (hair care, makeup, lotion, hygiene products, etc.) separately; make sure to label each box.

12. Keep a travel set ready to go and stored in your luggage. As a product runs low, replace it or refill it. No need to take up space in your bathroom with these items.
13. Wipe down cabinets, sinks, and your shower/tub—aka, CLEAN.
14. Put everything away in its designated container or drawer.
15. Throw out the trash.
16. Take any items you wish to donate to your place of choice.
17. Take expired medications to the local pharmacy for disposal.
18. Take "after" photos.

Tips for keeping your bathroom organized:

- Decide how many of each type of toiletry you need. I know you feel like you are getting a deal when you buy in bulk, but trust me, these items are always on sale. You don't need six tubes of toothpaste and five toothbrushes.
- Makeup does expire. Commit to what you use, then replace that. Throw out the rest.
- Resist samples. This is a marketing ploy to get you to be a consumer. If you have limited space, the last thing you need is tiny samples.
- Before purchasing any new product—shampoo, conditioner, or soap, for example—finish what you have. Even the shower can get cluttered.
- Stop bringing home hotel shampoos and conditioners. Use those when you are at the hotel. Instead, have your travel products filled and ready to go for each trip.

When your bathroom is organized . . . things my clients have said:

I can't believe it. My bathroom is clean. I didn't realize that all those empty bottles of shampoo, conditioner, and body wash had overtaken the bathroom. Once we threw them all away, well let's just say there was some serious yuck. Having all that clutter gone made it easy to clean. Imagine that, getting clean in a clean bathroom.

It got to the point that my bathroom vanity was filled with prescription bottles and yet I only take one medication. By clearing all of them out and dropping them off at Walgreens, I have to say I felt healthier. I can now keep my face cleanser, soap, lotion, and toothpaste there. The space feels less cluttered and is certainly easier to clean.

Easy let-go items:

Anything expired—meds, makeup, personal products.

Craziest thing I ever saw:

I had a client who kept his gun in the bathroom. If we are thinking about the intention of a room, I don't think guns have anything to do with what goes on in a bathroom—or at least I certainly hope not. We found a safe and secure place for him to keep his firearm in instead.

CHAPTER 9:

Living Room/Family Room

———⟨⟨⟨⟩———

For me this room is very special, as it is the space where all those living in the house can come together and share time—reading, playing games, watching TV, etc. With all those bodies sharing space, the less clutter the better. Ensuring that each item used in this room has a clear home helps to make the space "user-friendly"—meaning, everyone wants to use it!

Questions to answer:

1. What is your goal?
2. What is your intention for the space?
3. What is your deadline for completing the task?

Dear Andrea,
I think I have a problem.

Recently, a friend staged an "intervention" about my accumulation of twenty-five years' worth of stuff. Another friend flat-out said, "George, you need help." I consider myself to be capable, so I made an attempt to get organized. Now, in addition to all the stuff, I have piles in the middle of every room and I can't remember what's in them. You should know, I have had health issues for thirty-plus years, so my biggest concern is who will have to deal with my stuff when I die?

Did I tell you that I am a collector? Well, Andrea: I have watched enough episodes of the show *Hoarders* to know that no one wants to sort through this amount of someone else's stuff. Can you help? I would like you to help me prepare my house for my death.

In desperate need,
George

Not long after receiving that email, I met with George to address his concerns. I found that he, like so many people I meet, was more concerned about what other people thought than the negative impact the clutter has on the quality of his life. Too often we don't want to ask for help because we don't want to burden other people—which just prevents us from finding a way to change. I encouraged George to focus on why his friends felt so strongly about his need for help. Their concerns had to do with his safety and his overall well-being.

George's challenges were similar to those of others who have too much stuff: frustration at not being able to find something; irritation about the expense of repurchasing the same items; exhaustion from picking up over and over but never feeling any more organized; and, finally, embarrassment around other people seeing the mess.

Looking around George's home, I saw that he needed help. Picture a house that has been closed up for the season, with sheets covering everything. This was how George had tried to conceal his stuff. His library resembled an actual library, with rows and rows of books, but there were so many shelves that you couldn't see the individual titles. His bathroom cabinets held bottles upon bottles of expired medications. His closets included styles from the '70s, '80s, '90s, and early 2000s, with a range of sizes from medium to XXXL. The combined kitchen/living room had several shelves dedicated to various collections of tea sets, vases, DVDs, and CDs—all housed in shelving units also disguised with sheets. After taking a complete tour of the home, I could see why George talked about preparing for death; there was nothing in the house that reflected life.

So, where did we start? First, I asked George to identify which areas caused him the most stress (always attack the hardest areas first!). For George, that meant the piles covered with sheets in each room. Once we removed the sheets and addressed the piles one at a time, we were easily able to identify what he wanted to keep—and what I could take away.

I met with George for three hours every week for three months. After each of our organizing sessions, George would stand at the curb waving goodbye to me and my SUV filled with his stuff. And as we moved through the process, he began to thrive. He was thrilled with the result. On our last visit he said, "Andrea, I can't believe this is the same place. My home is beautiful. I am going to have a Christmas party and I want you to come." This was no longer a man preparing to die.

Six months later, George sold his San Francisco home, moved to Southern California, and bought a new condo. At the age of seventy-two, he is now dating. George reclaimed his life.

When we let go of the things that no longer serve us, we create space for new things to enter our world.

Organizing your living room/family room:

1. Take "before" photos.
2. Clean off your coffee table, side tables, and/or couch(es) to use for sorting and organizing.
3. Set up trash bags and donation bags and boxes.
4. Remove all items that do not fit the intention of the room.

5. Group "like" items into categories (books, games, blankets, etc.). Decide where everything should live.

6. Remove all electronic items that are no longer used and put in a box for either donation or e-waste.

7. Put books on bookshelves, and games in the gaming area.

8. If you like to have many blankets, consider having a trunk to store blankets and to use as a table.

9. Donate or toss outdated DVDs, videos, and CDs that you don't use.

10. Do the items you have on display and in drawers reflect your intention for the house and the family? If not, let them go.

Tips for keeping your living room/ family room organized:

- Everyone in the house should be responsible for the upkeep of these communal spaces. Keep a laundry basket nearby; use a rotating schedule so that at the end of the day someone is responsible for the redistributed items that have landed in the room. After that, pull the room together: pillows on couches, blankets folded, games and toys returned to their respective homes. Staying on top of it means exponentially less cleaning time in the long run.

- Typically the intention of this room is to be a gathering place for everyone in the home, so try to limit the amount of decorative stuff you keep in it room. I like to call this a "user-friendly" space, meaning you enjoy using the room, not cleaning it up.

- At the end of the day, leave the room how you would like to see it when you return.

When your living room is organized . . . things my clients have said:

It's Saturday night; my husband and I opted to stay in because we want to cozy up in what feels like a brand-new space! I love my house again!

In our house, we make it a game. Anyone that finds money in the couch, keeps it. I like that everyone is participating in keeping this organization going. There is a lot less fighting in our house. Thank you.

After a super hectic day, which is every day, I love that our living room is so inviting now that the clutter is all gone. We keep a laundry basket by the doorway and everyone is responsible for one day a week clearing the room of the stuff and putting those items where they belong. I no longer feel like I am the only one picking up stuff at the end of the day.

Easy let go item:

Old, no-longer-used electronic devices like DVD players!

Craziest thing I ever saw:

I had one client that hated having to go into the kitchen for drinks, so she'd added a small refrigerator next to her couch. Unfortunately, both of her refrigerators had gotten so full that she purchased a *third* refrigerator for the garage, which she'd also filled with food and drinks. We convinced her to let go of the living room refrigerator and replaced it with a small table and lamp that she now uses as her reading nook.

CHAPTER 10:

Guest Room

꧁ ❧ ꧂

Well this room really has no surprise meaning—it's a bedroom, for guests! So simple, and yet this space too often becomes a dumping ground for random stuff. If that is the case in your house, and you don't like it, I suggest you decide the intention of this room and from this point forward allow only items that align with that intention to live in this room.

Questions to answer:
1. What is your goal?
2. What is your intention for the space?
3. What is your deadline for completing the task?

Organizing your guest room:

1. Take "before" photos.
2. Set up trash bags and donation bags and boxes.
3. Ideally this room should have only items a guest who's staying over would need—a bed, a nightstand, and a dresser or closet where they can put their items. But as this is an extra room, it may have more than one purpose in your household. If that is the case, define the intention and designate a specific space where the items that fit the intention are stored.
4. Remove all items that do not fit the intention of the space.
5. Dispose of trash.
6. Put items you don't need, use, or want into your donation bags/boxes.
7. Take out your trash/bring your donations to a drop-off site.
8. Take "after" photos.

Tips for keeping your guest bedroom organized:

- Try not to have too many "intentions" for the guest bedroom. Keep it simple. Guests stay there. The end.
- Be careful about having too many things for your guests. Most people will have tooth-brushes, toothpaste, etc., with them. If they forget something, you can give them some of your toothpaste, and chances are you have extra toothbrushes from past visits to the

dentist. Don't burden your guests with stuff. They are here for you, not your gifts.

When your guest bedroom is organized . . . things my clients have said:

I can finally have guests stay here!

In the time of COVID, we needed our guest room to quarantine. It was nice to have a place to recover and not have to look at all the crap that used to be in here.

Easy let-go item:

All of the just-in-case guest stuff . . . you know, all the backup stuff you keep on hand for guests, from toothpaste to toothbrushes to soaps and lotion. These are not necessary. Sure, hold on to one extra toothbrush—that's a nice thing to be able to provide if someone's forgotten theirs—but everything else you can let go of. You are not a pharmacy.

Craziest thing I ever saw:

I had a client that felt the need to have just-in-case gifts. Well, that small footprint of having just a couple of things turned into a guest closet filled to the brim with stuff. To me, these gifts have no true meaning. Gifts should be specific to the individual they're for—something you've thought about, not "Oh I have this thing in a closet and I feel obligated to give this person *something*, so I'll just give them this." If the latter is what you're doing, then just skip the practice of must-give gifts. Also, if you find you have become a person who is frequently complaining about all the stuff they own, then stop doing that to other people by giving them stuff they don't need! In my book, the best gift is no gift. Instead, do something with the person—share an experience, like going for a walk or seeing a movie. No one needs another candle.

CHAPTER 11:

Laundry Room

———— ❧ ————

A h, just like the guest room, this room has a very clear definition. We all know what this one is for, so first and foremost, make sure yours is set up to allow you to complete the task of doing the laundry. If there's room for other things, you can consider storing them in this room, but those should all be secondary to its actual function. First and foremost, create a space where clothes can be washed, dried, and folded, and then— drum roll, please—taken directly out to be put away!

Questions to answer:

1. What is your goal?
2. What is your intention for the space?
3. What is your deadline for completing the task?

Dear Andrea,
I want to get my home and my life organized but I am worried that means I will have to throw everything away. Is that true? I am not sure I am ready to do that.
Signed,
Not sure I am ready

Dear Not Sure,
Are we ever really ready? I have found in my many years working as a professional organizer that one of the biggest stumbling blocks to getting organized is this fear of letting go, even if what you are holding on to is not working. As humans, we seemed to be hard-wired to want to hold on to everything. If I am being honest with you, yes, I would love it if my clients agreed to let go of "all the stuff," but I know my love of minimalism is not for everyone. So my first step in working with a new client is to determine what their hopes around getting their home organized are. Is it that they want to be able to sit down at their dining room table (which is currently covered in papers) and have a family dinner, find out what's going on with their kids? Is it they would like to park their car in the garage? Is it because they want to find something they lost? Is it that the energy of the house feels crazy because of all the stuff that's piled up?

Once I have the answers to those questions I work with the person to figure out what the best way to achieve that goal is. Sometimes that means things will leave the house. But I do not walk into someone's house with the thought, *I can't wait to throw all this out.* Instead, we consider what the intention of each space is, and whether the items in the space meet that need. It is through this decision-making process that my clients can decide what stays and what goes.

As for the actual organizing process, I do my very best to not throw things away but instead to find new homes for them . . . books get donated to libraries, blankets get donated to shelters, clothes get donated to people reentering the workforce. Sometimes knowing that the things you're parting with will have another life and be used makes it a little bit easier to let go.

I hope this helps to ease some of your anxiety.

Best,

Andrea

Organizing your laundry room:

1. Take "before" photos.
2. Set up trash bags and donation bags and boxes.
3. If you have counter surface, clear it off to use for sorting. If you don't, set up a folding table or some other flat surface to use
4. Pull out everything from cabinets and drawers.
5. Group like items into categories—e.g., detergents, house supplies, hardware.
6. Remove all items that do not fit the intention of the room.

7. Consolidate contents of partly used bottles.
8. Remove empty containers and put them in the trash.
9. Throw out any broken or damaged items.
10. Remove all items that you no longer use and put them in donation bags.
11. Wipe down cabinets, surfaces, and laundry machines.
12. Create specific zones for each category: house supplies, laundry supplies, hardware, etc.
13. Put small loose items in clear, labeled containers.
14. Put items away according to their category.
15. Empty the trash.
16. Take "after" photos.

Tips for keeping your laundry room organized:

- Every month, go through your products and dispose of the ones you don't use, then wipe down your machines and clean the rest of the space.
- Every week, match up all mismatched socks.
- When doing the laundry, complete the entire cycle: wash, dry, fold, and put away.
- Have a laundry cart with three sorting bags—light, medium, and dark. When a bag is full, it is time to do the wash.
- Have only one backup container of detergent. Laundry detergent can take up a lot of space—so instead of many bottles, do not have more than two at a time.

When your laundry room is organized . . . things my clients have said:

This room was our dumping room for everything. You couldn't tell what was dirty/clean laundry because of all the other stuff. But now that all that stuff is gone, there is no distraction. If there is a basket filled with clothes, it means laundry needs to be done. Laundry is not as much of a chore anymore, and we even have space to fold the clothes once they come out of the dryer.

The room is no longer a safety hazard . . . aka no more random stuff . . . so our kids are learning how to do their laundry.

Easy let-go item:

The bag of single socks that have never found a match.

Craziest thing I ever saw:

One client had lived in her house for over forty years and had a large laundry room with built-in cabinets, and yet she kept her detergent containers on top of the machines. When I inquired why she didn't use the cabinets, she said they were too full. So I opened one up—and sure enough, they were stuffed with old containers, including brands of detergents that no longer exist! In addition to all that unusable detergent, there were two dead rats in the cabinets. (Yes, we tossed those out too.)

CHAPTER 12:

The Garage

————◦◈◦————

Garages are meant to house vehicles—but I suspect your garage, like most people's, serves all sorts of purposes, from holiday storage to food storage to sports equipment storage. The key word here? *Storage*. This section will guide you on how to create specific zones for all these items so that your garage space is used efficiently and you always know how to locate what you're looking for.

Questions to answer:

1. What is your goal?
2. What is your intention for the space?
3. What is your deadline for completing the task?

Dear Andrea,
Can't believe it is already November. My twelve-year-old daughter wants to start decorating for Christmas—thank you, box stores, for starting your holiday decorations in October. Anyway, for the last two years she and I have been arguing about which stocking to hang. I want to hang the stocking her grandmother made and she wants to hang the pink and purple sparkle unicorn stocking she got at a birthday party. I know this is not a big problem but we seem to have more and more fights around it.
Thanks,
Mom of Tween

Dear Mom of Tween,
It's simple: Hang both! I am a big believer in what you have, you should use. In this instance, you have two stockings—so why not hang both of them? Now, you can be a bit cheeky and put her real stocking gifts in the handmade one and some good old-fashioned charcoal in the pink-and-purple sparkle one, but I will leave those shenanigans up to you. And don't forget—with the coming and going of the holidays, January 1 is a great time to put your home on a diet and let go of some of the stuff that has been cluttering up your house. Before you put all of those holiday decorations away, ask yourself if there are any you can now let go of . . . the ones you didn't use at all for instance! And hey,

by letting those go you have already achieved a common New Year's resolution: to lose weight. I believe letting go of stuff is the best weight loss program around!
Happy organizing,
Andrea

Organizing your garage:

1. Take "before" photos.
2. Set up trash bags and donation bags and boxes.
3. Remove any obstacles—cars, bikes—to open up a clear area for sorting and purging.
4. Pull everything out and group into categories: house supplies, hardware, sporting goods, power tools, holiday, etc. Yes, it gets worse before it gets better.
5. From each category, pull items that can be tossed.
6. Put remaining "keep" items in large clear Sterilite containers labeled with masking tape. I find yellow masking tape and a dark Sharpie pen a good choice for labeling, since the yellow is easy to spot even in a dimly lit space.
7. Now that you know the footprint of each category, decide where each should live and label those areas like a supermarket labels its aisles—e.g., Holiday, Sports, Camping. That way everyone will know where things should be put away after use.
8. Optimize the space in your garage by utilizing metal shelving. You don't need to spend a ton of money on this. Just go to your local hardware

store and purchase some easy-to-assemble shelves, ideally ones that go from floor to ceiling.

9. Put your newly labeled bins on the shelves you've designated for them.
10. Sweep the garage floor.
11. Toss out your garbage.
12. Take your donation items to charity shops.
13. Take "after" photos.

Tips for keeping your garage organized:

- Food that's kept in a garage often gets forgotten about, and goes unused. Is it really necessary to store any food in the garage? Now that you have cleaned out your kitchen, you should have enough space in there for all your food—which is where edible items should live!

- Holiday stuff: Have a set space where your holiday-related items live so the amount you have cannot exceed the space. At the end of every holiday, if there are items that you did not use, donate them.

- Keepsakes: Have a set area where you keep them, and come up with a long-term plan for their use: Are you going to look at this item regularly? Are you keeping this other thing to give to someone? If your keepsakes sit in a storage bin with no intention, what is the point of keeping them?

- Paint: Dried-up cans should be tossed. (Keep in mind that paint can be toxic and dangerous to the environment if it's not disposed of properly, so if there's still any paint in there, look up how to handle it responsibly.) Take pictures of empty paint cans in case you need to match those colors in the future. Drop off any unused cans at your local paint store.

When your garage is organized . . . things my clients have said:

I feel like we could move at a moment's notice—not that we're going anywhere, but I love this lighter feeling!

I love the fact that my garage is practically empty! There's so much room in there now that it just feels better. I know exactly what's in every box because I can see it.

I no longer over-purchase house supplies, because I now have one shelf in my garage that I shop from when I run out of something in the house.

Easy let-go item:

Anything that is damaged and/or broken.

Craziest thing I ever saw:

Expired emergency food dated 1979. I don't think that stuff was safe to consume even in the most dire of circumstances. That food went straight into the trash.

CHAPTER 13:

Home Office

⁕

The home office always has a special place in my heart in terms of organizing . . . as this is the room where my business got its start. I was working part time doing basic home accounting, and one day I inquired of a client, "Why do you keep dog food in your office?" That led to many other questions about their overall home setup, and from there my home organizing business began.

Questions to answer:
1. What is your goal?
2. What is your intention for the space?
3. What is your deadline for completing the task?

Organizing your home office:

1. Take a "before" photo.
2. Clear off your desk so you can use it as a space for sorting.
3. Set up trash bags and donation bags and boxes.
4. Pull out all loose paperwork, books, and office supplies.
5. Group like items into categories.
6. Remove any items that do not fit the intention of the space.
7. Sort paperwork into three categories: file, to-do, and shred.
8. Deal with your paperwork! I know it stinks but this is your chance to get it done.
9. Remove any equipment that is no longer used—calculators, printers, computers—and put it all in bins for donation.
10. Put everything away according to category.
11. Throw out trash. For electronics, many stores now accept e-waste so research your area for locations, dates and times for drop off.
12. Drop off your donation items.
13. Take "after" photos.

How to handle paperwork:

When it comes to paperwork, the biggest question for many people is, "What do I keep?" This is why setting an intention is so important. Make a list of essential documents, gather those together, and decide on a set place for them—preferably a fireproof safe.

Must-keep items:

- Birth certificates
- Social Security cards
- Marriage license
- ID cards
- Passports
- Life insurance policies
- Investment policies
- Legal papers
- Estate planning documents
- Divorce agreement
- Vehicle titles
- House deed
- Mortgage deed
- Tax returns for the past seven years

Organizing your paperwork:

1. Gather all of your paperwork.
2. Using the list above, decide what paperwork you need to keep and what you can toss.
3. Group all like documents that you intend to save.
4. Sort the "keep" pile by year (you want to make this process simple), then label clear bins with each year and put the documents in their correct bins.
5. Discard the rest of the papers via recycling or shredding them. If doing the shredding yourself is too much, there are many services, including ones that can come to your home, that you can hire to help you.

6. Make magazines manageable. If they are stacking up, put your subscriptions on hold until you get through the current issues.
7. Keep only books that you regularly use in your home office.

Organizing your mail/email:

1. Unsubscribe from all lists that send emails you don't read.
2. Unsubscribe from catalogs.
3. Decide where your paperwork should live, and then keep it there.
4. Have a station where all mail goes when it comes in. I like the acronym ARF—action, recycle, file. So, in your entryway, or wherever you tend to put your mail, have two trays— one for action and one for filing—and put a bin on the ground next to them for recycling.

Tips for keeping your mail/email organized:

- Deal with mail in real time, or at least daily.
- Toss catalogs. Consider this a money saver: what you don't see, you don't buy.
- Convert any bills you're still receiving via snail mail to electronic bills.
- Scan paper piles to digital files to reduce the amount of paperwork you have and to make things you absolutely need more accessible.

When your office is organized . . .
things my clients have said:

Organizing the office was daunting because of all the papers. Once I got through it all, I realized I no longer need paper bills and converted everything to online. With less paper, the room is more inviting and I am working in my home office rather than sitting on the couch.

Easy let-go item:

Excess office supplies.

Craziest thing I have ever seen:

I had a client who saved all charity mail that he received in hopes that at the end of the year he would go through it all at the same time and decide then which charity to support. A lot of the charities attach coins, nickels, and quarters to their mail; after going through it all, he had an extra $1,000—not bad!

CHAPTER 14:

Child's Bedroom

———◦♣◦———

I have a very specific reason for creating a separate category for your child's bedroom: I believe this room is one more opportunity to teach your child important life lessons, from figuring out who they are and how they want to express themselves to how to take care of the things that are important to them. I think it is a great way to model what kids learn in school, too—things like "when you finish using something, you put it away" and "if you really like something, you take care of it." And we all know having a neat room helps improve sleep, which in turn improves learning . . . all positives for growing kids!

I've organized this chapter a little differently than the others in this part of the book, since there are so many factors at play in a space meant for kids. You'll see what I mean as you work your way through!

Questions to answer:

1. What is your goal?
2. What is your intention for the space?
3. What is your deadline for completing the task?

Organizing your child's bedroom:

1. Take "before" photos.
2. Set up trash bags and donation bags and boxes.
3. Clear off their bed so you can use it as a sorting space.
4. Start with the clothes: take out all their clothes and group them into categories—shirts, pants, jackets, sweaters, shoes, etc..
5. Pull all clothes that are damaged or permanently stained and throw them away.
6. Pull all clothes that no longer fit but are in good shape and decide whether they should be donated or held on to for one of your younger children. Put the clothes you've decided to keep in a clear bin, with sizes clearly labeled, and put the bins away (see tips below for how to ensure you don't forget about these!).
7. Put the clothes that you're keeping and that your child will wear now in their proper places.
8. Throw out the trash.
9. Take donation items to a drop-off site.
10. Take "after" photos.

Tips for keeping your children's clothes organized:

- Divide up the clothes that don't currently fit but that you want to keep into sizes and then store them in clear containers (one for each size). Keep the containers in an area that can be the "store" where you can shop as your child grows. *Put a reminder on your calendar* to bring out the next size of clothes as your child gets bigger. It's easy to forget about this stash—and then, before you know it, your child has grown bigger than the size of the clothes you have stored and all that effort's been for nothing.

- You may have friends with older kids who declutter their closets regularly and then donate to you. But just because someone has given clothes to you doesn't mean you a) have to accept it, and b) have to keep it even if you did initially accept it. They are doing exactly what you are doing: emptying out their home of stuff they don't need.

- Find a family shelter that accepts donations of the kinds of items you're purging. This may help ease some of your worries about letting go of things associated with your child. Plus, when your child sees the importance of giving to others, they may want to practice giving away other items that they no longer need or want— books, toys, video games, and so on. Instead of "that's mine" thinking, your child may develop "how can I help other kids?" thinking.

- Get a dresser, and set it up in a way that will help them learn how to put their clothes away. It is a simple and very effective way to teach a good habit. Top drawer(s), underwear and socks; middle drawer(s), shirts; bottom drawer(s), pants. Children like to be a part of the overall planning of their rooms. If your child can't read yet, a simple picture and a masking tape strip with the word on the outside of each drawer can help.
- Three times a year, go through your children's clothes to "purge": at the beginning of the school year; after Christmas; and at the end of the school year. As new things come in, old things must go out.
- Have a two-section laundry bin, and at the end of the day play the "toss the dirty clothes in the correct bin" game.

Tips on keeping your child's bedroom organized:

- Make the bedroom a low-stimulus room. Create a place for your child to wind down with only a bed, a couple of books, and a desk.
- Don't story *anything* under the bed. Out of sight often means out of mind and out of use.
- Only items that belong to your children should live in their bedroom, if at all possible.
- Sometimes your children's room will have more than one intention; if that's the case, designate zones for each purpose — reading area, play area, and so on. Be careful not to over-stuff each area.

- Teach your children how to put things away and then practice doing so daily. Just like at school, there is a time to use something and a time to put something away. A great tool is having a clock in the room and establishing ahead of time that at a certain time, things are put away. The more you get your kids involved in the upkeep of your house, the less you will have to do.

Tips on organizing children's artwork:

- Designate a single area where your kids' art is displayed.
- Rotate the art as new pieces come in.
- As you rotate the art, decide which pieces you will keep and put them in a clear labeled bin. Once that bin gets full, instead of buying a new bin, go through and reconsider what you are keeping.
- To reduce the footprint of what you are keeping, consider the possibility of digitizing the art. There are several services that will turn your children's artwork into photo books.

Tips on organizing children's books:

- Have a set area where your children's books live—ideally a bookshelf.
- As your child grows out of the books, donate them to your library.
- Sign your child up with a library card so that they take ownership and learn to return what they borrow.

- Have one set area for book returns.
- Put "trip to the library" on your family calendar as a recurring event. This can be a fun, free experience for the whole family. We don't need to own everything.

Tip on organizing children's keepsakes:

- Have one clear labeled bin for each child. At the end of the school year, go through the keepsake bin with your child to determine the best items to keep. Your child may surprise you and not want to keep all the items that you have put in there over the years.

Tips on organizing children's toys:

- Ideally, keep toys in one area.
- Limit the number of toys you keep based on the size of the chosen area.
- Toys can take over the home. Children often have so many toys that they no longer play with everything they have. So, create an incentive plan for them to earn toys using a calendar and a point system. The more expensive the toy, the more points are needed to purchase it . . . for example, a yo-yo might be 2 points, whereas a drum set could be 200 points. It's amazing what can happen as kids learn to work for what they want. That yo-yo may no longer be of interest once they know they are working toward something bigger. And you don't have to stop there—instead

of a purchasing a toy, perhaps they can earn points to purchase an experience, like going on a vacation to Disney.

- Sort through toys three times a year: at the beginning of the school year, after the first of the year, and at the end of the school year. Donate usable items to family shelters and children's hospitals. Include your children in this activity; as they begin learn the act of giving to others, it will plant the seeds for letting go of things they no longer need, use, or love, and teach them that life is not about having all the stuff!

- In some homes, LEGO displays take over. Remember, they are toys and can be reused. After the structure your child has built has been displayed for an agreed-upon time, have a breakdown party day and then encourage your child to create something else using their imagination.

- At the end of playtime, toys are put away. Model what kids do at school. Many teachers set aside a specific amount of time in which kids are expected to put toys away. You can do this too!

- Stop giving out birthday party gift bags to kids that come to your child's birthday party. Every parent struggles with too much stuff—it's not just you. Consider talking to the other parents and agreeing to put an end to this very unnecessary habit.

- If you're trying to be eco-conscious, stop purchasing plastic toys.

Children's responsibilities:

At a young age, start giving your child chores, like making the bed, to complete at home. This can be as simple as pulling the blanket up over the bed. The perfectly made bed is not the point; it is that the made bed sets the stage for a clean room.

Maintain a rule that nothing can be left on the bedroom floor at the end of the day. Things must be put away before bed.

Designate spots for your kids' jackets, backpacks, and school papers. Make sure that they put each thing in its proper place when they come home, and eventually you won't have to oversee the process anymore—it will become habit.

Chores you can assign to your kids at home:

- Clearing the dining table
- Putting dishes in the dishwasher
- Helping with the laundry (if they know how to operate a video game, they can understand how to turn on the washing machine)
- Feeding the pets
- Wiping down counters
- Picking up the family and living rooms at the end of the day
- Putting toys away
- A great one for teenagers is cleaning the bathroom. Teens *love* being in the bathroom; since they spend so much time in there, it shouldn't be hard for them to take a few minutes each day to pick up towels and wipe down the counter, sink, and shower.

Bottom line:

Everyone living under the same roof should participate in the upkeep—including your kids!

When your kids are organized . . . things my clients have said:

The best outcome of this organizing experience was my son's report card, which came out the quarter after Andrea helped us learn to organize. The teacher stated that organizational skills are an area of strength for our son! The quarter prior, organizational skills were identified as an area for improvement. This happened because the whole family got organized together. Including your kids in the process is the key to success.

The quality of our family life has improved tenfold after learning how to be organized. Previously, I found myself falling deep into depression. So much improved after Andrea taught us how to organize that I sat down and made some resolutions for the new year that I have, for once, been able to accomplish. This expense originally felt indulgent but honestly, it was the best money we have ever spent. No regrets here. I just can't say enough good things about the whole experience!

Easy let-go item:

Any piece of clothing about which your child says, "I don't like it." Life is short, and I am sure your kid has many other options. Listen to them and let it go.

Craziest thing I ever saw:

A four-year-old child had 220 pairs of shoes. We lined them up on the outside deck and took a picture from above. I kept thinking that at four years old, this child's foot was likely growing so fast that by the time we finished taking the photo the shoes might no longer fit.

CHAPTER 15:

Organizing by Category

———————— ⚜ ————————

W e have gone room by room, so now let's look at organizing by category.

Organizing your electronics:

1. Get all your electronics together and attach the matching charging cords.
2. Put all remaining charging cords that do not have a matching device into a donation bag.
3. Donate any device that you don't use. If you are concerned about privacy, use the factory reset button before donating. Several stores, like Whole Foods, have donation days during the year when they accept e-waste.
4. Every person in your house should have a box, labeled with their name, for their devices and chargers. If you are old enough to have a device then you are old enough to be responsible for

it . . . and divvying up things this way will significantly cut down on the "that's my charger" fights in your household.

Organizing old media:

1. Donate. Donate. Donate.
2. If you no longer have the devices to play these items that are taking up space in your house (DVD players, VCRs, record players, etc.), then you absolutely *must* donate them!

Organizing books:

1. Create a home library. Get simple bookshelves and put all of your books on them. This doesn't have to be expensive; you can find inexpensive new shelves at IKEA, and used shelves for even cheaper on Craigslist and Facebook Marketplace.
2. Try not to mix too many decorative items with your books. It gives a cluttered feeling. Remember . . . what is the intention of a bookshelf? You get the idea.
3. Regularly peruse your bookshelves and donate the books you are not going back to read. Again. Many libraries will sell the books you've donated and put the funds back into the library system.
4. Get a library card. Less stuff = less time organizing. In addition to paper books, you can reserve audiobooks through the library system.

Organizing your photos:

1. Get all your photos and albums together.
2. Sort the photos by dates and events.
3. Send duplicates to your friends and family.
4. Consider scanning your photos and getting rid of the physical versions of all but your favorites.
5. Store loose photos in clear containers and label the outside of each container based on date, friend group, or event.
6. Decide on one location where all your photos will live, and keep them there.

Organizing keepsakes:

1. Every once in a while, take out all of your keepsakes, take a look at them, and consider the importance of why you want to keep them, where you store them, and how you store them. I know we love our keepsakes, but too often we store them in places like garages and basements—which I believe devalues the meaning behind keeping them. So, if you must have keepsakes, be intentional about how and where you will store them.
2. If you are keeping something that has a purpose—e.g., pieces of fine China, crystal, or silver, for example—try using them instead of storing them. Some people say they worry about breaking items, but does that matter if they are never used?
3. Decorative keepsakes—pick a place in your home where you can display the keepsakes

and every once in a while—perhaps at the start of a new season—rotate the display.

4. Have a plan for your keepsakes for after you die. Thinking about exactly who will get what will help you to determine whether you really need to keep each item—and perhaps you could even give some of those things to the people they're meant for now!

Hello Andrea,

I wanted to inquire about your services. I'm trying to help my in-laws downsize to a smaller house. They're in their early seventies, and have been living in the same house for twenty-plus years. At this stage in their lives, it's a bigger home than they need, and as retirees, it is no longer financially viable for them to stay there.

They've been talking about moving for the last eight years but seem stuck on how to move forward. Not only does it seem physically daunting, it also feels emotionally challenging. It seems they may need some kind of mediator or therapist to help them get through the decision-making. Is this something you do? If not, is there someone you could recommend? Thank you.

Signed,

Organized Challenged

Dear Organized Challenged,

Thank you for contacting me. My first suggestion, before you hire anyone to help, is to help your in-laws get in the mindset of "it's time to downsize." If they are not on board, you won't be successful, and any attempts to force them to move forward will likely make the situation worse. One suggestion is to consult with their primary care doctor. Their generation grew up with a "Do what your doctor says" attitude, so I suggest your wife gets permission to call their doctor to discuss their fears surrounding a move and the benefits of downsizing—financially, physically, and emotionally.

Next, start thinking about ways that the move can be an asset to their lives. From my own experience with my ninety-three-year-old mother, one of the hardest things about aging is that things are constantly being taken away—from the physical stuff to decisions about where to live. I like the approach of figuring out the positives. Perhaps you can start looking at options for where they could live next. Right now they fear the unknown, but if you could find something they like perhaps they would see that this is not the end of their lives, just an exciting new chapter.

Lastly, check out professional organizers in your area to see if you can find anyone who has helped clients similar to your in-laws. Sometimes getting an outside professional's perspective can shift the thought process on downsizing and moving. The key will be helping them to see the possibility of improvement to their quality of life.

Best,

Andrea

Organizing your linens:

1. Group all of your linens into sets.
2. Have one extra set for each bed—no more!
3. Get rid of mismatched sets, along with any that you don't use, love, or need.
4. Donate extras to your local animal shelter.
5. To save space, put folded sheet sets inside a matching pillow case and store vertically on shelf or flat in a drawer.

Organizing House Supplies:

1. Group all your supplies together by category—paper products, batteries, light bulbs, toiletries, etc.
2. Store each category in one designated location. This way you'll always be able to find what you are looking for and will reduce duplicate purchases of things like paper towels, because you'll know what you already have. This will also help you know when it is truly necessary to replace items.
3. Put delivery subscriptions on hold and go through your backstock of supplies.
4. Be careful of buying in bulk. If you don't have room for it, don't buy it.

Organizing luggage/travel items:

1. Pull all your luggage out.
2. Are there any bags that you don't use? Donate them. Fill those pieces of luggage with other donated items from the house.

3. Decide where all remaining luggage should live.
4. Nest smaller bags in larger bags to save on storage space.
5. Store travel toiletries, neck pillows, and other travel items in your luggage. When you unpack, make note of any item that needs replacing.

Organizing your collections:

1. Do you collect some things on purpose? Mugs? Key chains? How are you using or displaying them? If you are never using them—and especially if they are sitting in a storage bin in your garage—perhaps it is time to stop collecting these items and give them away.
2. Are you known for liking something specific— a certain animal, for example? If so, do you often receive items related to that animal as gifts? If you're done with feeling like you have too much stuff, it is time to let your friends and family know that you are getting organized and to please stop with the frog-themed gifts. (And if you are guilty of doing this yourself, this is your wakeup call to stop cluttering someone else's life!)

Organizing gifts:

1. I can't tell you how many people I know who have limited space but still have an area dedicated to "just in case I need to give a gift." No more just-in-case gifts!

2. If you are giving a gift, before buying any-
    thing, really think about the person and their
    wants and needs. Consider providing an expe-
    rience, such as tickets to an event, rather than
    buying or making a physical present. My
    favorite thing to do is to ask my friends to
    pick a date and then decide on something we
    can do together.

3. You do not need a closetful of wrapping sup-
    plies. If you are limited on space, this is your
    obvious let-go-of practice. Instead, can you
    be creative by using something you already
    have? I like to use last month's kitchen cal-
    endar. This is your chance to reuse what you
    already have and to free up some space.

Organizing your shopping:

1. Never go shopping without a list—especially
    at the big stores like IKEA, Target, Costco,
    and Walmart, where you can walk in thinking
    you are buying one item and then walk out
    with a cart full of stuff—and strive to stick to
    that list.

2. Get what you need when you need it. Unless
    you are living in a rural place, you do not need
    to stockpile things like dish soap and shampoo.
    You can see when things are getting low and
    replace them before they run out.

3. Turn your computer off at night—no late-night
    online shopping.

4. Don't buy something just because it is on sale.
    You don't need to buy twenty rolls of paper

towels because they are on sale. If it is on sale now, it will most likely be on sale again. Have you ever walked into Macy's and not seen a sale sign?

5. Practice mindful shopping: When you are making a purchase, ask yourself, *What is the intention of this purchase?* Is your answer valid? If not, don't make the purchase.

6. Make a rule: When one purchased item comes into the house, one item must go out (if you are feeling extra courageous, make it *two* items that must go!).

7. Use all of your wrapping paper, tissue paper, and boxes before you get anything new.

8. If you receive mail orders or internet orders, as soon as the item arrives, break down the packaging and put it in your recycling bin.

9. No sample products: You know those sample products they like to give you when you purchase something at a department store? Please resist; don't bring those items home. I had one client who could never say no and had more than 2,000 beauty sample items at home. If you want to start learning how to stay organized, learning to say "no thank you" will be vital to your success.

Managing grandparents:

1. Grandparents want to give things to their grandchildren. But you and your partner may not want all that stuff. Give your parents redirection on how they can contribute to the

family. Keep an ongoing list of your family's needs so you are prepared to give them suggestions when birthdays or holidays come around.

2. Set up a fund grandparents can contribute to—for college, summer camp, a tutor, a family vacation, or, best of all, a trip to visit the grandparents! Grandparents want to make a genuine contribution to your family; you just need to tell them how.

3. Not all grandparents will initially be on board with the "no gifts" rule, so you may need to have a real heart-to-heart conversation and share with them how all that stuff is overwhelming and leads to stress and disorganization in your household.

Organizing shared spaces:

Whether you share space with roommates, a partner, and/or children, these are some helpful guidelines for everyone:

1. Have a chore calendar that rotates and stick to it. I like to keep ours on the refrigerator door.

2. When you leave a room, make sure you're leaving it the way you found it.

3. Have a monthly dinner with everyone in your household at which you discuss which systems are working and which are not.

4. Photograph each organized room and find a place where you can subtly display it. That is the goal that everyone who lives in the house must agree to try to live up to.

PART III:

Some Final Tips

CHAPTER 16:

Avoid the Common Mistakes

1. **Getting supplies prior to starting the job.** Don't start by getting storage containers. Reduce the volume of your stuff first, *then* decide if you need containers. Also, take a walk around your house to see if there is anything you can use that will serve the same purpose as a container.

2. **Burdening others with your stuff.** When getting rid of stuff, resist the "Oh, I should give this to my friend" urge. It all comes back to intention. Why are you giving your things away? Because you want less stuff. So before you decide that the stuff you're purging should go to friends or family, ask yourself, *Does this person want or need this item any more than I do?* Don't

burden others with the very things you know *you* should get rid of. If you think that someone needs something, ask them first; otherwise, find an organization that will benefit from your donation.

3. **Blaming everyone else for the mess.** Don't worry about other household members' stuff; focus on organizing *your* things first.

4. **Making piles.** Don't leave stuff on the floor; it just attracts more stuff.

5. **Hiding things.** Don't shove things in closets and drawers. When you choose to put something in a particular space, do so with clear intention: that is where the item should live, along with similar items.

6. **Focusing on the fear.** Instead of focusing on the "what ifs," focus on your ideal outcome. What is that for you? Being able to find your car keys or to sleep in a clutter-free room?

7. **Obsessing over perfection.** Instead of thinking your house has to be perfect, strive for "good enough"; once you declutter, you may be surprised to find that it's actually better than perfect, because it's clutter-free!

8. **Thinking you are the only one who can organize.** Do you feel the need to do this all yourself? If you live with other people, nip

this feeling in the bud! Everyone in your household should be part of the process of keeping your home organized.

9. **Keeping things, just in case.** If you are overwhelmed by all the stuff surrounding you, stop keeping things JUST IN CASE. Live in the present moment, use what you have, and wait until something starts to run out before replacing it.

10. **Storing things in many places.** I liken this behavior—storing backup supplies like lightbulbs, toothpaste, and bags in many places because we think we should keep the items nearest to where they are used—to acting like a squirrel. Hey, unless you are living in a twenty-bedroom mansion, nothing is that far away. And when we store stuff all over, we lose track of what we have and end up either over-purchasing those products or running out because we assume we must have that thing *somewhere* in the house. Instead of falling prey to this trap, pick one place to store items. When something runs out, you'll know exactly where your backup is—and when you use that backup, you'll know it's time to replace the stock. Less stuff. Less purchasing. Saving money. Wins all around.

11. **Don't complete the job.** The most important rule of organizing is to finish what you've started. Even if you have to break up the

project into several days, always finish the project; never just end midway through. After each organizing session, put the room back together—don't leave it a chaotic mess.

CHAPTER 17:

Where Does It All Go?

⸻ ❦ ⸻

I often hear, "I don't just want my stuff going to just *anyone*; I want it to go to someone good." Okay, sure, that sounds nice—but if you are feeling totally over-whelmed by your stuff, help yourself out: go ahead and assume that everyone is good.

You may want to sell your goods; if you can, do it. But if your goal is just to simply get rid of the excess stuff weighing you down, then just donate everything and set yourself free!

Here are some of your options for making donations:

Goodwill:

They have the donation process down. Goodwill often has drive-up donation sites with large box contain-ers sorted by items. To expedite the process, prior to

97

drop-off, sort your goods according to their category: clothes, electronics, books, shoes, and household goods. Then you can just drive up, hand off your things, and drive off—super easy.

If you want to feel good about your donations, it might help you to know that Goodwill is actually doing good things in this world. According to their website, "Goodwill is an American nonprofit 501 organization that provides job training, employment placement services, and other community-based programs for people who have barriers to their employment."

Local charity shops that serve populations you support:

In California, we have a great organization called Under One Roof—a nonprofit retail store that raises millions every year for education and support services for men, women, and children living with HIV/AIDS. With just a little digging online, it shouldn't be hard to unearth a local non-profit organization that aligns with your values and accepts donations.

Craigslist "free stuff" page:

As I suggested in Chapter 2, if you post things here I suggest that you set a deadline for what you've put out and then follow up after to make sure everything has gone away.

Facebook community pages:

I have posted pics of all sorts of items, from recycled wood to baby clothes, on my community's Facebook page, and they all have been scooped up. Remember that saying, "One man's trash is another man's treasure"? Turns out that often rings true!

Great organizations that can also take your stuff:

- ASPCA
- Dress for Success
- Habitat for Humanity
- One Warm Coat
- Out of the Closet
- Salvation Army
- St. Anthony's
- St. Vincent de Paul Soles4Soles
- The Arc
- Vietnam Veterans for America

Also, make sure to check out your local food banks, libraries, hospitals, daycare centers and shelters for their current list of needs.

CHAPTER 18

Maintenance

———— ❦ ————

Daily:

1. First thing in the morning, make your bed and put clothes away.
2. After every meal, wash the dishes and clean off your counters.
3. Create an evening routine before everyone goes to bed—fold blankets, put away toys, put dirty clothes in the laundry bin and dishes in the dishwasher.
4. Leave rooms how you want to find them the next time you enter them.
5. A new item comes in, an old item goes out. Put the old item in a donation bag.
6. Go through mail. Create three piles—toss, action, file. Toss papers go into recycling. Action pile is added to the calendar. File papers go into your "office area."

Weekly:

1. Take out the trash, recycling, and compost.
2. Go through your two mail trays ("action" and "file"). The more frequently you do this, the less overwhelming the paper maintenance will be.
3. Do laundry and put it away . . . and yes, children after a certain age can be responsible for their laundry. Remember if they can navigate the cell phone, they can navigate the laundry machines.
4. Clean bathrooms.
5. Drop off donation bag(s).

Yearly:

1. At the end of each school year go through children's clothes to determine what they have outgrown and either pass those clothes on to another child in the house or donate them. Adults should take this opportunity to go through their own clothes and get rid of what is damaged, doesn't fit, or isn't being worn.
2. On birthdays and holidays, remember the new-items-in, old-items-out rule.
3. During tax time, grab the bin you stored your paperwork from eight years ago in and shred those papers (yes, they can go!) and then relabel that bin with the current year's date.
4. On the first day of every new season, do a scan of your clothes for the previous season and pull any items you did not wear.

5. Go through you keepsake bins to either rotate new items into use/display or weed things out for donation.

6. Go room to room and ask yourself, *Does this room need to be organized?* (Might be a good time to take this book out and go through your checklist of what to do!)

The End is Just
the Beginning

———— ❧ ————

Working as an organizer for so many years, I have had the pleasure of seeing firsthand what organizing can do to change someone's life: A five-year-old who said she felt like a new person after getting her room organized. A seven-year-old who stopped wetting his bed. A man who thought that by organizing his home, he was preparing for his death, but ended up selling that home, moving to a new city, and beginning to date (shout-out to George!). A widowed father who needed to reorganize the home for just he and his son after losing his wife to breast cancer.

This is powerful stuff.

Personally, having less stuff frees me up to live the life I want—one that is not about cleaning and organizing and feeling overwhelmed. I believe when we take notice of our stuff, we can choose what serves us and release the things that have no place in our lives. In letting go, we make room for what's possible.

In every chapter of this book, I asked you what your intention for taking on this project was. Once you have the answer that works for you, you are ready to get to work. The bottom line is simple: we have too much stuff. So once you know the answer to that question, ask yourself the next bigger and better question—what can you let go? I hope this book becomes your user's manual to help you get out from underneath that mountain of stuff and set you free of clutter.

If the process still feels overwhelming, don't be shy. Ask for help—from the other people who live in your house, a close friend, or, even better, a professional organizer. Having been in this business for fifteen years, I know how getting the help you need can change your life for the better.

Take care, and happy organizing!

About the Author

Andrea launched Andrea Wait Organizing Services in 2009 because she's always been drawn to helping people and because she absolutely loves organization. Yes, *loves*. There are endless ways to design spaces that improve not only functionality but also mental clarity and physical wellness. She know firsthand the difference it makes to have your space designed around what you really need. Decluttering opens up so much more than just a space—it opens up opportunity.

Andrea has been organizing ever since she was a child, but she really started to understand its impact as an adult. Her reduce/recycle approach has served her well everywhere she's lived—from the sprawling sub-urbs of Long Island to space-challenged apartments in Manhattan and finally to San Francisco, where years of shared-living situations made her an expert in managing space and inventory.

Though her work is focused on the Bay Area, Andrea has had the great fortune to travel around the country working with homeowners, business owners, renters, and landlords, each time discovering something new in the process of discussing their unique challenges. She feels privileged to have been invited into people's lives to help them make changes and she hopes that this book can reach countless more, aiding as many people as possible in creating the home of their dreams.

Made in the USA
Middletown, DE
05 December 2023

44722825R00070